Lerner SPORTS™

GREATEST OF ALL TIME PLAYERS

G.O.A.T. FOOTBALL TIGHT ENDS

Josh Anderson

T0018694

Lerner Publications ◆ Minneapolis

SPORTS THRILLS MEET RESEARCH SKILLS

Lerner SPORTS

Free Database Trial: lernersports.com

Lerner Publications Company
An imprint of Lerner Publishing Group, Inc.
241 First Avenue North
Minneapolis, MN 55401 USA

For reading levels and more information, look up this title at www.lernerbooks.com.

Main body text set in Aptifer Sans LT Pro.
Typeface provided by Linotype AG.

Library of Congress Cataloging-in-Publication Data

Names: Anderson, Josh, author.
Title: G.O.A.T. football tight ends / written by Josh Anderson.
Other titles: Greatest of all time football tight ends
Description: Minneapolis, MN : Lerner Publications, [2024] | Series: Lerner sports. Greatest of all time players | Includes bibliographical references and index. | Audience: Ages 7–11 years | Audience: Grades 2–3 | Summary: "From protecting the quarterback to catching a touchdown pass, tight ends can do it all. See how the top 10 tight ends in football history rank. Then rank them yourself!"— Provided by publisher.
Identifiers: LCCN 2023012380 (print) | LCCN 2023012381 (ebook) | ISBN 9798765610213 (lib. bdg.) | ISBN 9798765623596 (pbk) | ISBN 9798765614822 (epub)
Subjects: LCSH: Tight ends (Football)—United States—Biography—Juvenile literature. | Football players—United States—Rating of—Juvenile literature. | BISAC: JUVENILE NONFICTION / Biography & Autobiography / Sports & Recreation
Classification: LCC GV939.A1 A529 20241 (print) | LCC GV939.A1 (ebook) | DDC 796.332092/2 [B]—dc23/ eng/20230515

LC record available at https://lccn.loc.gov/2023012380
LC ebook record available at https://lccn.loc.gov/2023012381

Manufactured in the United States of America
1 – CG – 12/15/23

TABLE OF CONTENTS

PLACES WITH MANY JOBS   4

PLAYERS WITH MANY JOBS   4

FACTS AT A GLANCE   5

No.10 GREG OLSEN   8

No.9 KELLEN WINSLOW   10

No.8 JASON WITTEN   12

No.7 OZZIE NEWSOME   14

No.6 SHANNON SHARPE   16

No.5 ROB GRONKOWSKI   18

No.4 MIKE DITKA   20

No.3 ANTONIO GATES   22

No.2 TRAVIS KELCE   24

No.1 TONY GONZALEZ   26

EVEN MORE G.O.A.T.   28

YOUR G.O.A.T.   29

GLOSSARY   30

LEARN MORE   31

INDEX   32

PLAYERS WITH MANY JOBS

The Tampa Bay Buccaneers were playing the Kansas City Chiefs in the 2021 Super Bowl. The Buccaneers wanted to build on their 7–3 lead in the second quarter. Tampa Bay tight end Rob "Gronk" Gronkowski was on the edge of the offensive line. From this position, a tight end can either block or go out to catch a pass.

FACTS AT A GLANCE

» A TIGHT END HAS NEVER WON THE NATIONAL FOOTBALL LEAGUE (NFL) MOST VALUABLE PLAYER (MVP) AWARD.

» TONY GONZALEZ RANKS THIRD ALL-TIME WITH 1,325 CATCHES. HE SPENT HIS CAREER WITH THE KANSAS CITY CHIEFS AND THE ATLANTA FALCONS.

» KELLEN WINSLOW OF THE SAN DIEGO CHARGERS LED THE NFL IN CATCHES IN 1980 AND 1981.

» ROB GRONKOWSKI WON THREE SUPER BOWLS PLAYING WITH THE NEW ENGLAND PATRIOTS AND ONE WITH THE TAMPA BAY BUCCANEERS.

The play started, and Gronk headed toward the end zone. A Chiefs defender grabbed him as he ran. The referee threw a penalty flag. Defenders may not hold receivers as they try to make a catch.

Gronk is no ordinary player. His speed and strength made him one of the best tight ends ever to play the game. He broke away from the defender holding him. Seconds later, he caught a 17-yard throw from Tampa Bay quarterback Tom Brady for the touchdown. The Buccaneers took a 14–3 lead.

Tight ends have many jobs. On running plays, they need to be powerful blockers. They help create holes in the defense for their team's running backs to run through. On passing plays, tight ends help protect the quarterback. They block fast and strong defenders seeking a sack. Other times, tight

Cowboys tight end Jason Witten (*left*) blocks Philadelphia Eagles defender Malcolm Jenkins (*right*) in a 2017 game.

Chiefs tight end Travis Kelce runs toward the end zone with the ball.

ends run out to catch passes. The best tight ends are strong blockers, fast runners, and skilled pass catchers. Although no tight end has ever won the NFL MVP award, they are key members of a team's offense.

The Chicago Bears picked Greg Olsen in the first round of the 2007 NFL Draft. He was the first tight end chosen that year. Since 2007, NFL teams have chosen only 13 other tight ends in the first round.

Olsen played nine of his 14 NFL seasons for the Carolina Panthers. He led the Panthers in receiving yards three times, including in 2015. The team went 15–1 and made it to the

Super Bowl that season. They lost to the Denver Broncos.

From 2011 to 2019, Olsen was a favorite target of Panthers quarterback Cam Newton. The two connected for 36 touchdowns during their time together. Olsen and Newton hooked up for more than 1,000 receiving yards in a season three times.

After retiring after the 2020 season, Olsen became an NFL announcer on TV. In 2023, he announced the Super Bowl between the Philadelphia Eagles and the Kansas City Chiefs.

GREG OLSEN STATS

Catches	742
Receiving Yards	8,683
Touchdown Catches	60
Pro Bowls	3

KELLEN WINSLOW

Kellen Winslow was a leading pass catcher in the NFL in the 1980s. He played during a time when most tight ends did more blocking than receiving. Winslow played all nine of his NFL seasons for the San Diego Chargers.

A coach once said Winslow looked like an offensive lineman but played like a wide receiver. The coach meant Winslow had the speed and skill of a receiver and the big, strong body of an offensive lineman. That made him very difficult to tackle.

Winslow led the NFL in catches in 1980 and 1981. Since then, a tight end has only led the league in catches three times. Winslow gained more than 1,000 receiving yards three times during his career.

The NFL picked Winslow for its 100th Anniversary All-Time Team. The team included the greatest players of the league's first 100 years. In 1995, he became a member of the Pro Football Hall of Fame.

KELLEN WINSLOW STATS

Catches	541
Receiving Yards	6,741
Touchdown Catches	45
Pro Bowls	5

One of the greatest tight ends in NFL history began his college football career as a defender. When Jason Witten decided to play for the University of Tennessee after high school, he planned to play on the defensive line. But with the team's top tight end injured, Witten took his place on the field. He set school records for catches and receiving yards by a tight end.

In 2003, the Dallas Cowboys drafted Witten. He played for the Cowboys for 16 seasons. Witten ranks fourth all-time among NFL players with 1,228 career catches. And his 13,046 receiving yards rank second all-time among tight ends. Witten helped lead the Cowboys to the playoffs six times. He finished with more than 1,000 receiving yards four times. After his NFL career, Witten turned down both college and NFL coaching jobs so he could coach at the school his children attended in Texas.

JASON WITTEN STATS

🏈	Catches	1,228
🏈	Receiving Yards	13,046
🏈	Touchdown Catches	74
🏈	Pro Bowls	11

OZZIE NEWSOME

Ozzie Newsome played 13 seasons in the NFL, all for the Cleveland Browns. He led the Browns in receiving yards every season from 1981 to 1985. Newsome finished his career as Cleveland's all-time leader in catches and receiving yards. He ranks ninth among all tight ends with

7,980 receiving yards.

He never played in the Super Bowl, but Newsome helped lead the Browns to the playoffs seven times. In three of those seasons, the team reached the American Football Conference (AFC) Championship game.

After his playing career, Newsome spent 17 seasons as the general manager of the Baltimore Ravens. General managers do many jobs for NFL teams, including hiring coaches and choosing new players. Newsome joined the Pro Football Hall of Fame in 1999.

OZZIE NEWSOME STATS

Catches	662
Receiving Yards	7,980
Touchdown Catches	47
Pro Bowls	3

SHANNON SHARPE

Shannon Sharpe is one of the greatest tight ends of all time, but some fans argue that he wasn't even the best player in his own family. Sharpe's older brother, Sterling Sharpe, was a five-time Pro Bowl wide receiver for the Green Bay Packers. But Shannon Sharpe's NFL career stats are better, and he played nearly twice as many seasons as his older brother played.

Shannon Sharpe was a key part of the Denver Broncos offense that led the team to back-to-back Super Bowl victories in 1998 and 1999. Sharpe and legendary quarterback John Elway connected 41 times for touchdowns during their years as teammates.

Sharpe led the Broncos in receiving yards six times. He ranks fifth all-time among tight ends with 10,060 receiving yards. After his playing career, Sharpe achieved something his brother did not. He joined the Pro Football Hall of Fame in 2011.

SHANNON SHARPE STATS

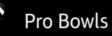 Catches	815
Receiving Yards	10,060
Touchdown Catches	62
Pro Bowls	8

ROB GRONKOWSKI

Rob Gronkowski was a fan favorite during his playing career. In addition to playing in the Super Bowl six times, Gronk entertains fans off the field. In 2018, he swam with tiger sharks during Discovery Channel's Shark Week. He has also competed in pro wrestling matches and comments on football games on TV.

In the NFL, Gronkowski finished with more than 1,000 receiving yards four times and ranks 12th all-time with 92 touchdown catches. In 2011, he led the league with 17 touchdown catches.

Gronkowski won three Super Bowls during nine seasons with the New England Patriots. After retiring from the NFL for the first time in 2018, he came back to win another Super Bowl with the Tampa Bay Buccaneers in 2020. He retired for good after the 2021 season.

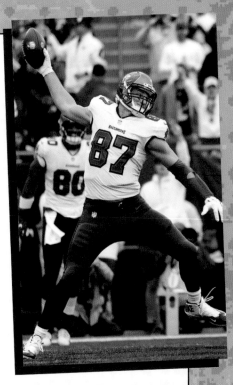

ROB GRONKOWSKI STATS

Catches	621
Receiving Yards	9,286
Touchdown Catches	92
Pro Bowls	5

MIKE DITKA

Mike Ditka helped change the tight end position. He played for the Chicago Bears and other teams during the 1960s and 1970s. Before then, tight ends were used mainly as blockers, not pass catchers. But Bears coach George Halas used Ditka as a main target in the team's passing attack. Ditka's toughness and strength helped him become a strong blocker as well.

Ditka played six of his 12 NFL seasons for the Bears. He led the team in receiving three times, including in 1963. That year, the Bears won the NFL Championship. The NFL Championship was the top prize in football before the Super Bowl began in 1967.

After his playing career ended, Ditka became head coach for the Bears. He led the Bears to victory in the 1986 Super Bowl. He also coached the New Orleans Saints. Ditka joined the Pro Football Hall of Fame in 1988.

MIKE DITKA STATS

Catches	427
Receiving Yards	5,812
Touchdown Catches	43
Pro Bowls	5

ANTONIO GATES

Antonio Gates took an odd route to the NFL. Unlike most NFL players, he didn't play college football. Instead, he played college basketball at Eastern Michigan and Kent State. But many National Basketball Association teams thought he wasn't tall enough to play pro basketball. So the 6 feet 4 (1.9 m) Gates decided to try out for NFL teams instead. His first tryout was with the San Diego Chargers, and he soon joined the team.

Gates played for the Chargers for his entire career, moving with the team from San Diego, California, to Los Angeles, California. He helped lead the Chargers to the playoffs seven times, including a trip to the AFC Championship in 2008.

Gates is the team's all-time leader in catches, touchdown catches, and receiving yards. His 116 touchdown catches rank seventh all-time among NFL players. No tight end has caught more touchdowns than Gates did.

ANTONIO GATES STATS

Catches	955
Receiving Yards	11,841
Touchdown Catches	116
Pro Bowls	8

TRAVIS KELCE

After playing college football at the University of Cincinnati, Travis Kelce joined the Kansas City Chiefs in 2013. Kansas City picked him in the third round of the NFL Draft.

In his first nine seasons in the league, Kelce gained more than 1,000 yards seven times. That's more 1,000-yard seasons than any other tight end has had in NFL history. He has led the Chiefs in receiving five times. Kelce already ranks fourth among all tight ends in league history in catches and receiving yards. He has been a Pro Bowl player every season from 2015 to 2022.

Kelce and quarterback Patrick Mahomes have teamed up to make Kansas City's offense one of the best in the NFL. Mahomes became the team's starting quarterback in 2018. Since Mahomes and Kelce began playing together, the Chiefs have reached the AFC Championship game every year and won the Super Bowl in 2020 and 2023.

TRAVIS KELCE STATS

Catches	814
Receiving Yards	10,344
Touchdown Catches	69
Pro Bowls	8

Stats are accurate through the 2022 NFL season.

TONY GONZALEZ

Most tight ends can't match the pass-catching stats of wide receivers. Tight ends usually spend too much time blocking to catch a lot of passes. But tight end Tony Gonzalez stacks up against even the most legendary wide receivers who have played in the NFL.

Gonzalez spent 12 years playing for the Kansas City Chiefs. He finished his career with five seasons with the Atlanta

Falcons. He ranks third all-time in the NFL with 1,325 catches. He ranks sixth with 15,127 receiving yards. And he's eighth in touchdown catches with 111. His 14 Pro Bowls are tied for second-most all-time.

Gonzalez was also famous for something he didn't often do. After fumbling five times in his first three seasons, he only fumbled once in his remaining 14 seasons. That's incredible for a player who touched the ball as often as Gonzalez did.

Gonzalez has worked as a football announcer since his playing career ended in 2013. In 2019, he joined the Pro Football Hall of Fame.

TONY GONZALEZ STATS

Catches	1,325
Receiving Yards	15,127
Touchdown Catches	111
Pro Bowls	14

EVEN MORE G.O.A.T.

There have been so many amazing tight ends throughout football history. Choosing only 10 is a challenge. Here are 10 others to consider for your G.O.A.T. list.

....

No. 11	RUSS FRANCIS
No. 12	JACKIE SMITH
No. 13	JOHN MACKEY
No. 14	CHARLIE SANDERS
No. 15	DAVE CASPER
No. 16	JERRY SMITH
No. 17	BEN COATES
No. 18	JIMMY GRAHAM
No. 19	VERNON DAVIS
No. 20	MARK BAVARO

YOUR
G.O.A.T.

It's your turn to make a tight end G.O.A.T. list. If some of your favorite players don't play tight end, make a list for another position too! You can also make G.O.A.T. lists for movies, books, and other things you like.

Start by doing research. You can check out the Learn More section on page 31. The books and websites listed there will help you learn more about football players of the past and present. You can also search online for even more information about great players.

Once you have your list, ask friends and family to create their lists. Compare them and see how they differ. Do your friends have different opinions about the greatest players? Talk it over and decide whose G.O.A.T. list is your favorite.

GLOSSARY

American Football Conference (AFC) Championship: the championship game of one of the NFL's two conferences

announcer: a person who describes and comments on the action in a sports event

block: to push or get in the way of an opposing play

end zone: the area at each end of a football field where players score touchdowns

fumble: when a football player loses hold of the ball while handling or running with it

NFL Draft: a yearly event when NFL teams take turns choosing new players

offense: players on a football team who try to score

offensive line: the five players who line up in front of the quarterback and block defenders

Pro Bowl: the NFL's all-star game

running back: a player whose main job is to run with the ball

sack: when a defender tackles the quarterback for a loss of yards

wide receiver: a player whose main job is to catch passes

LEARN MORE

Goodman, Michael E. *Kansas City Chiefs*. Mankato, MN: Creative Education, 2023.

Levit, Joe. *Football's G.O.A.T.: Jim Brown, Tom Brady, and More*. Minneapolis: Lerner Publications, 2020.

NFL 100: Official All-Time Team Roster
https://www.nfl.com/100/all-time-team/roster

Pro Football Hall of Fame
https://www.profootballhof.com/

Sports Illustrated Kids: Football
https://www.sikids.com/football

Stabler, David. *Meet Travis Kelce: Kansas City Chiefs Superstar*. Minneapolis: Lerner Publications, 2024.

INDEX

AFC Championship, 15, 23, 25

Brady, Tom, 6

Carolina Panthers, 8–9
Chicago Bears, 8, 20–21
Cleveland Browns, 14–15

Elway, John, 17

Kansas City Chiefs, 4–5, 9, 24–26

Mahomes, Patrick, 25

New England Patriots, 5, 19
Newton, Cam, 9

Pro Bowl, 16, 25, 27
Pro Football Hall of Fame, 11, 15, 17, 21, 27

Sharpe, Sterling, 16, 17
Super Bowl, 4–5, 9, 15, 17–19, 21, 25

Tampa Bay Buccaneers, 4–6, 19

University of Tennessee, 12

PHOTO ACKNOWLEDGMENTS

Image credits: Kevin C. Cox/Staff/Getty Images, p.4; Patrick Smith/Staff/Getty Images, p.5; Icon Sportswire/Contributor/Getty Images, p.6; Jason Miller/Contributor/Getty Images, p.7; Al Bello/Staff/Getty Images, p.8; Streeter Lecka/Staff/Getty Images, p.9; Focus On Sport/Contributor/Getty Images, p.10; Focus On Sport/Contributor/Getty Images, p.11; Stacy Revere/Contributor/Getty Images, p.12; Richard Rodriguez/Stringer/Getty Images, p.13; Focus On Sport/Contributor/Getty Images, p.14; Focus On Sport/Contributor/Getty Images, p.15; Allen Kee/Contributor/Getty Images, p.16; Focus On Sport/Contributor/Getty Images, p.17; Abbie Parr/Stringer/Getty Images, p.18; Douglas P. DeFelice/Stringer/Getty Images, p.19; Bettmann/Contributor/Getty Images, p.20; Bettmann/Contributor/Getty Images, p.21; Rob Leiter/Contributor/Getty Images, p.22; Nick Laham/Staff/Getty Images, 23; Ronald Martinez/Staff/Getty Images, p.24; Jamie Squire/Staff/Getty Images, p.25; Robert B. Stanton/Stringer/Getty Images, p.26; Grant Halverson/Stringer/Getty Images, p.27

Cover: Icon Sportswire/Contributor/Getty Images; Stacy Revere/Contributor/Getty Images; Patrick Smith/Stringer/Getty Images